MAN

V.

LIVER

MAN

V.

LIVER

NEIL HINSON
PAUL FRIEDRICH

Andrews McMeel
Publishing, LLC
Kansas City • Sydney • London

Andrews McMeel Publishing, LLC
an Andrews McMeel Universal company
1130 Walnut Street, Kansas City, Missouri 64106

www.andrewsmcmeel.com

ManvLiver.com
ManvLiver@gmail.com

13 14 15 16 17 TEN 10 9 8 7 6 5 4 3 2 1

ISBN: 978-1-4494-3855-5

Library of Congress Control Number: 2013931050

ATTENTION: SCHOOLS AND BUSINESSES
Andrews McMeel books are available at quantity discounts with bulk purchase for educational, business, or sales promotional use. For information, please e-mail the Andrews McMeel Publishing Special Sales Department: specialsales@amuniversal.com

Dedicated to my liver.
Keep up the good work, champ!

Introductory Note

Everyone has that friend who keeps them out too late. Tries to turn a Tuesday happy hour into a Friday free-for-all. This friend will crack open your can of secrets with the simple formula of equal parts shots and beers. Repeat.

You laugh with this person into the night, maybe even share a slurry cab ride. But you heal from your hangover alone under the bright fluorescence of your next workday.

I am that friend. This is my battle.

Man v. Liver

I'M BORED, WHICH MAKES MY LIVER SHUDDER.

I'M AWASH IN
EXCITEMENT...
OH WAIT, THAT'S SWEAT.

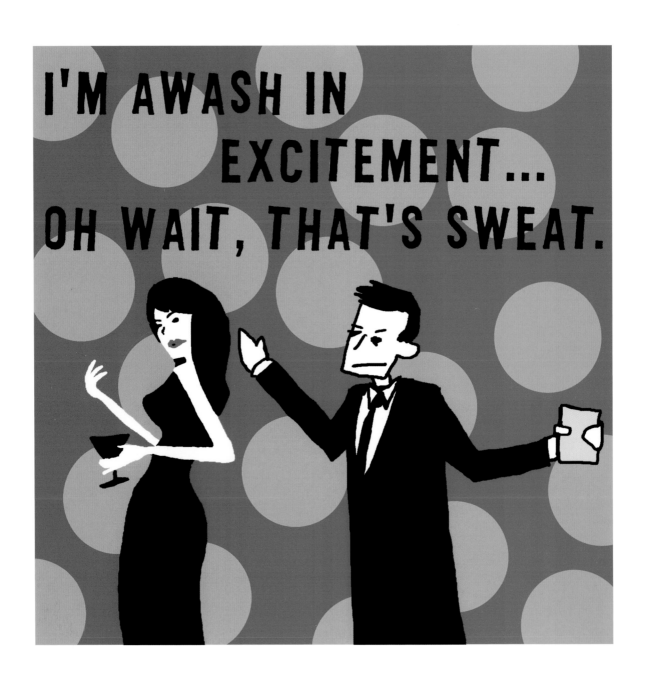

KNOW WHAT
MAKES A
GREAT
DRINKING GAME?

DRINKING.

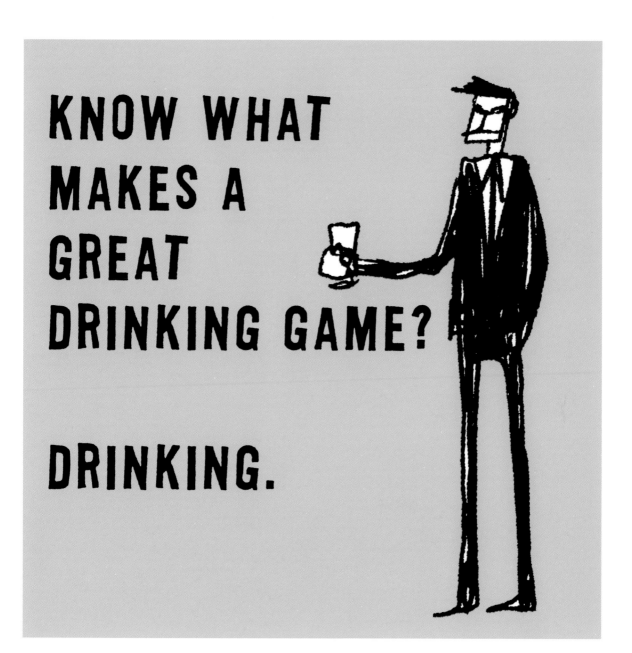

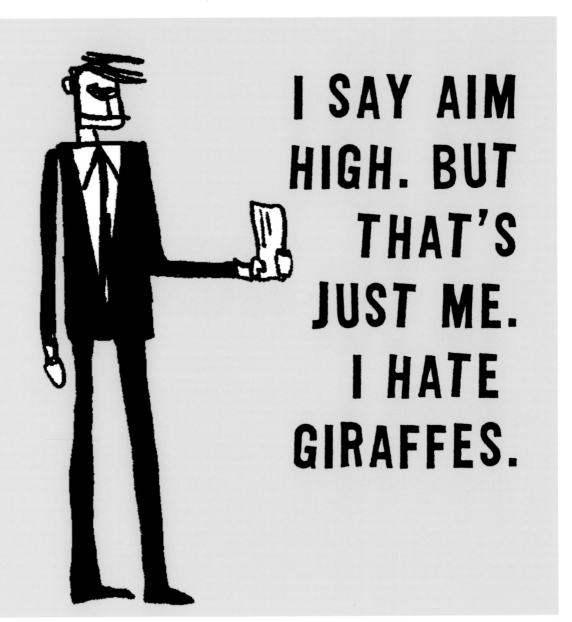

I SAY AIM HIGH. BUT THAT'S JUST ME. I HATE GIRAFFES.

COFFEE FOR ME, UNTIL NOT.

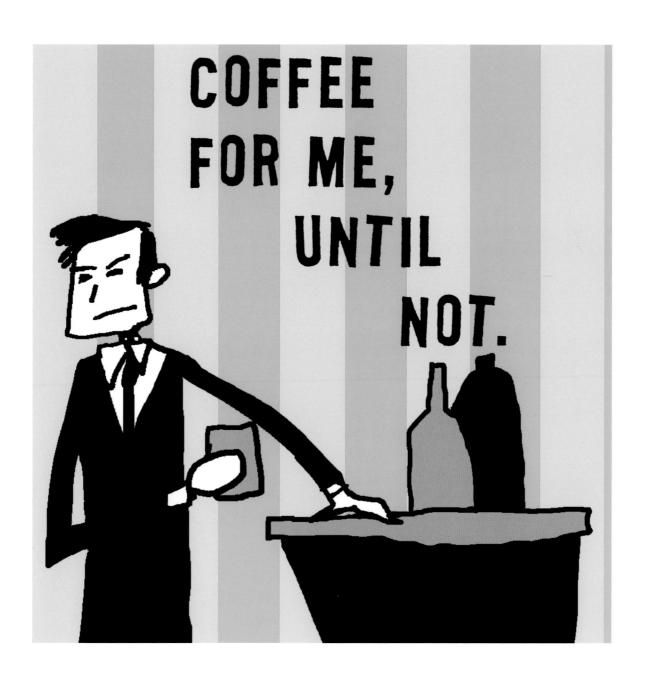

I'M OLD ENOUGH TO BE YOUR FATHER.
I'M YOUNG ENOUGH TO BE YOUR STEPMOTHER.

IF YOU'RE GOING
TO BE BAD,
LOOK GOOD
DOING IT.

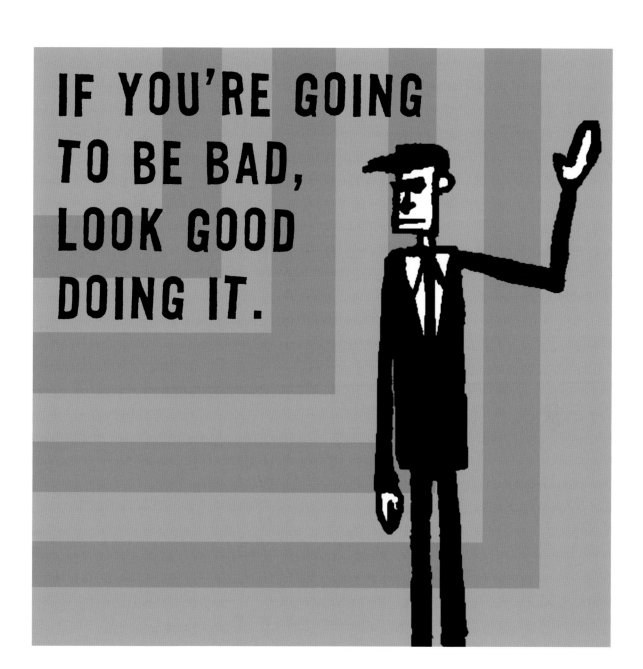

NOTHING LASTS FOREVER, DEAR.
NOT EVEN FOREVER.

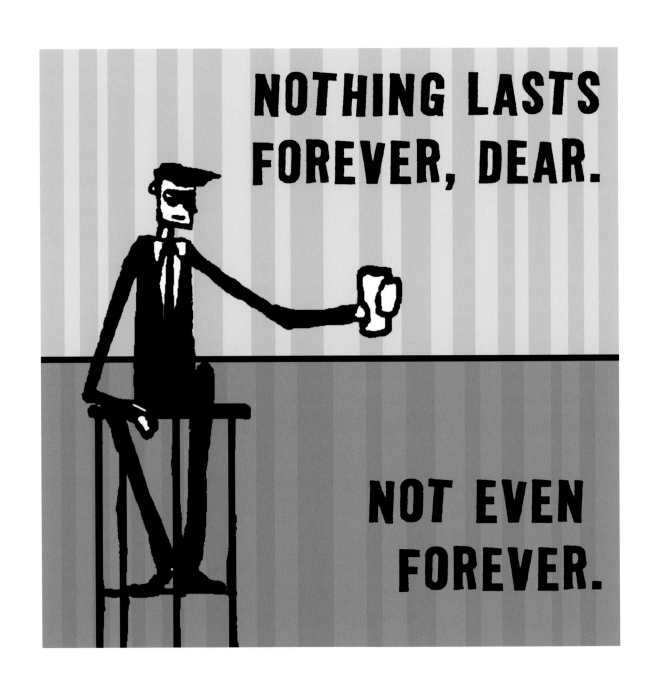

SLEPT IN MY CLOTHES LAST NIGHT. WHICH MEANS I WAS THE BEST-DRESSED AT BREAKFAST.

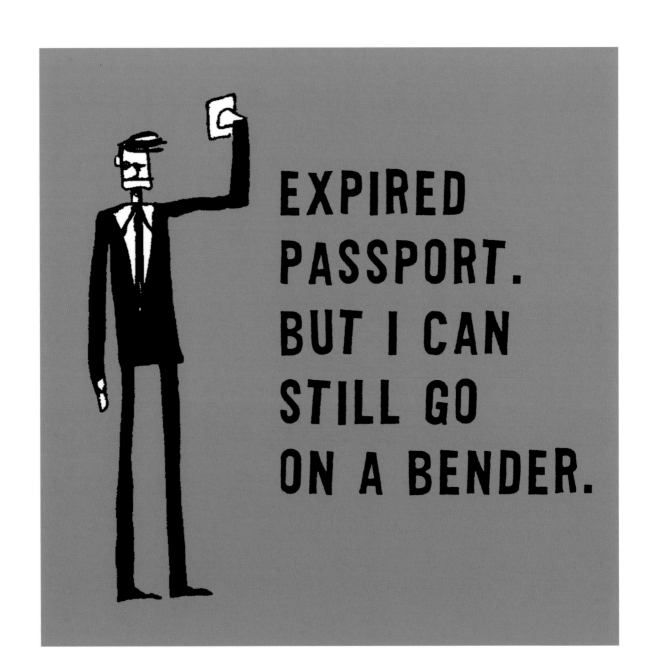

EXPIRED
PASSPORT.
BUT I CAN
STILL GO
ON A BENDER.

SCREW IT.
IT'S NOON
SOMEWHERE.

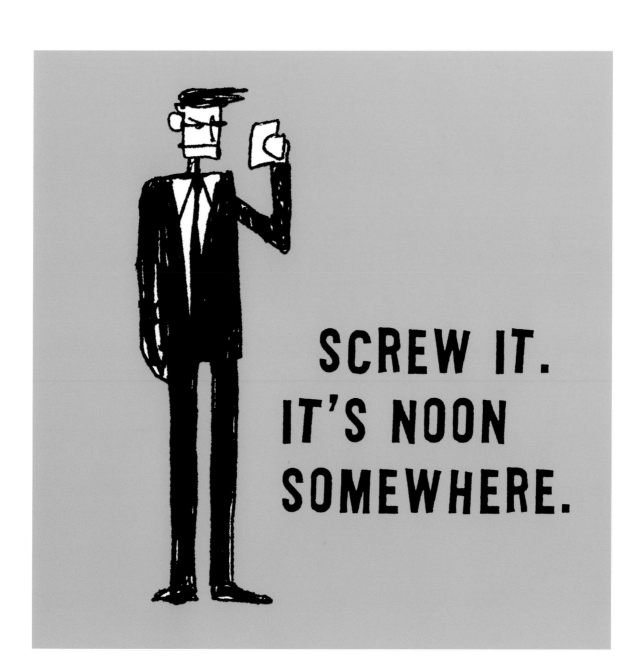

IF A TREE MAKES A
DOUBLE ALBUM
IN THE WOODS
DOES ANYONE
LISTEN TO IT?

DON'T
SAY
GOOD-BYE
WITHOUT
LEAVING.

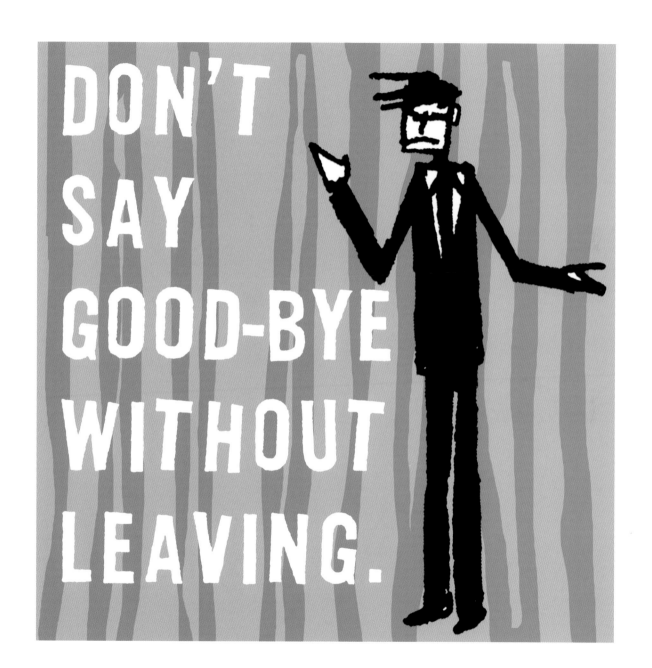

I'M READY FOR ANYTHING EXCEPT YOU.

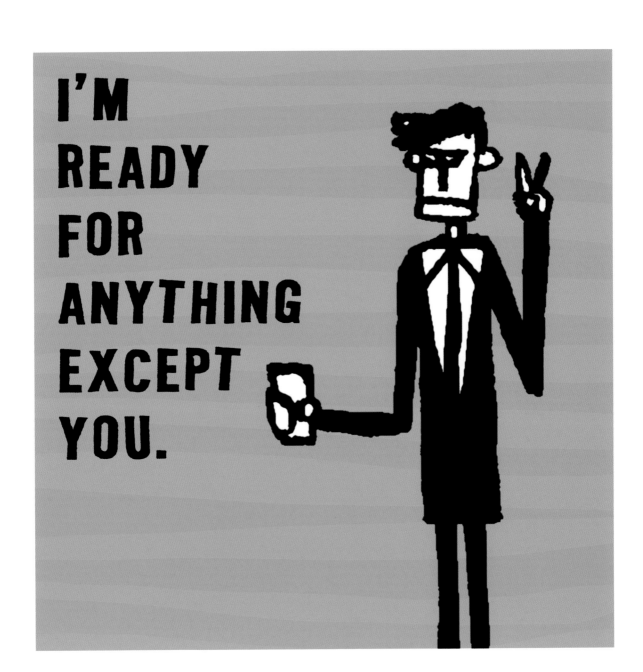

THESE PANTS ARE SCRATCH 'N' SNIFF.

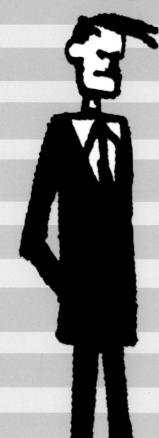

I DON'T THINK SHE
SAID TOPEKA.

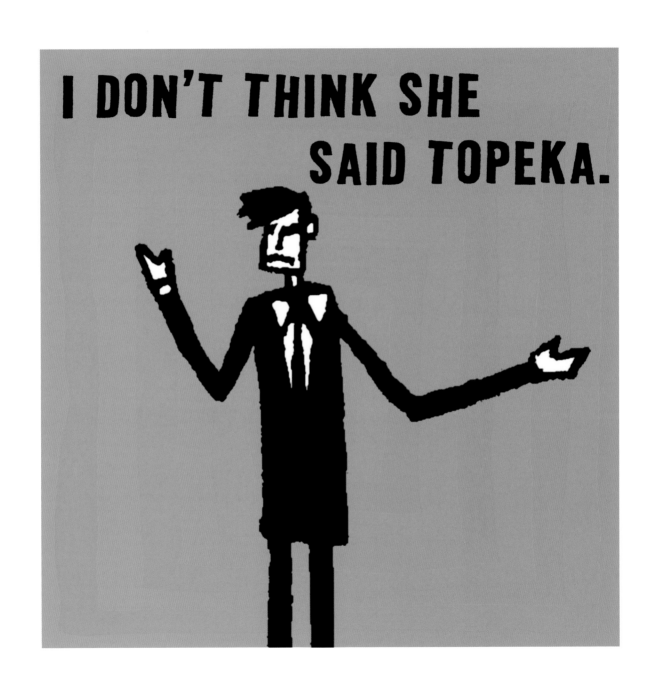

AM I BLURRING
MY WORDS?

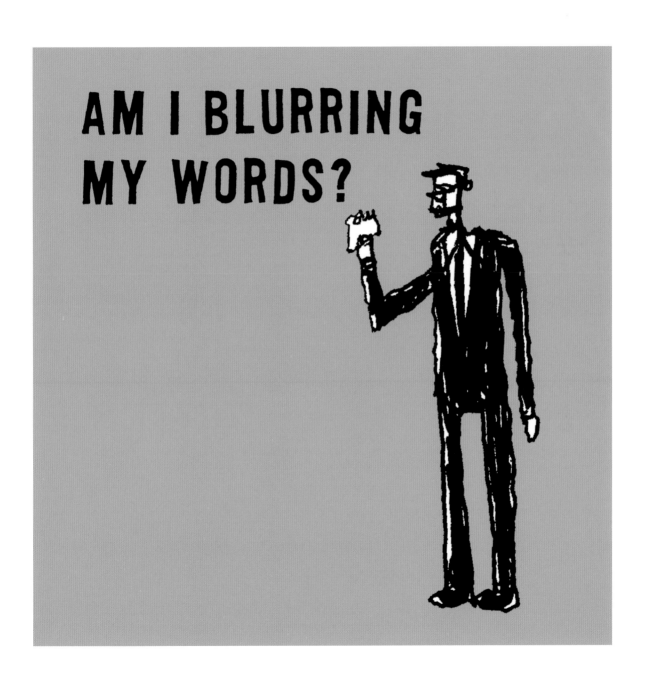

THIS IS WORTH
THE HANGOVER.

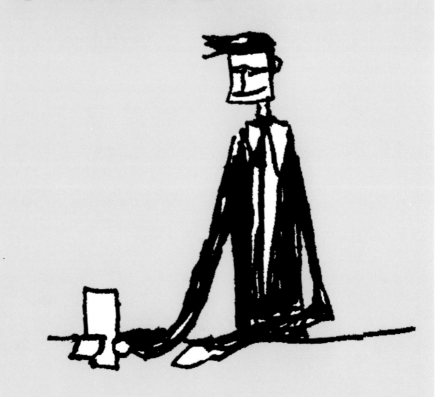

I LOVE WOMEN WHO
TALK ABOUT
CHOCOLATE
CATS
MIXED DRINKS
AND SHOES.

INSTEAD OF NEVER SPEAKING OF THIS AGAIN, LET'S JUST KEEP DRINKING 'TIL WE FORGET IT.

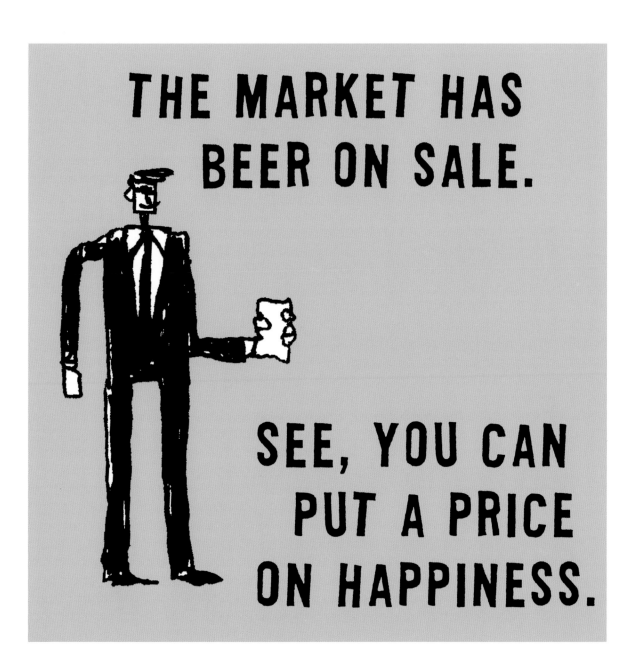

THE MARKET HAS
BEER ON SALE.

SEE, YOU CAN
PUT A PRICE
ON HAPPINESS.

QUIET PLEASE.
HANGOVER
IN PROGRESS.

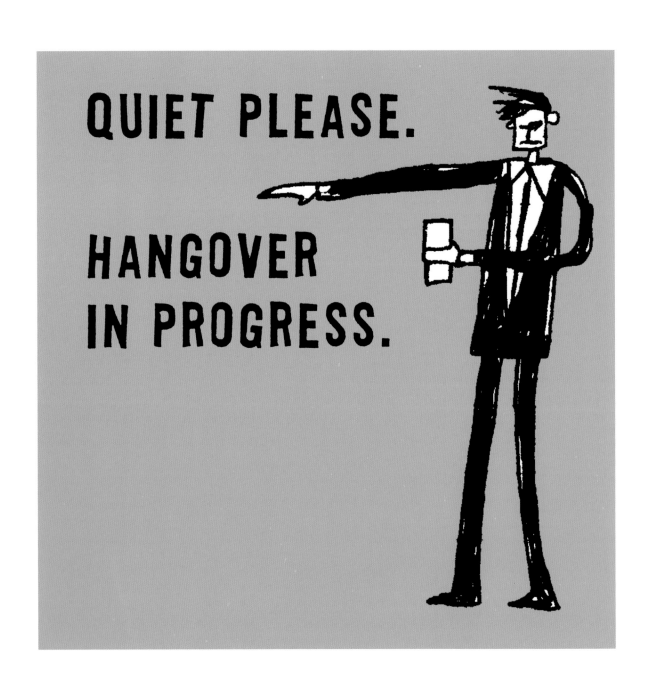

I'M BLANKING ON YOUR NAME BUT I REMEMBER YOUR DRINK. AND THAT'S WHAT'S IMPORTANT. TO ME.

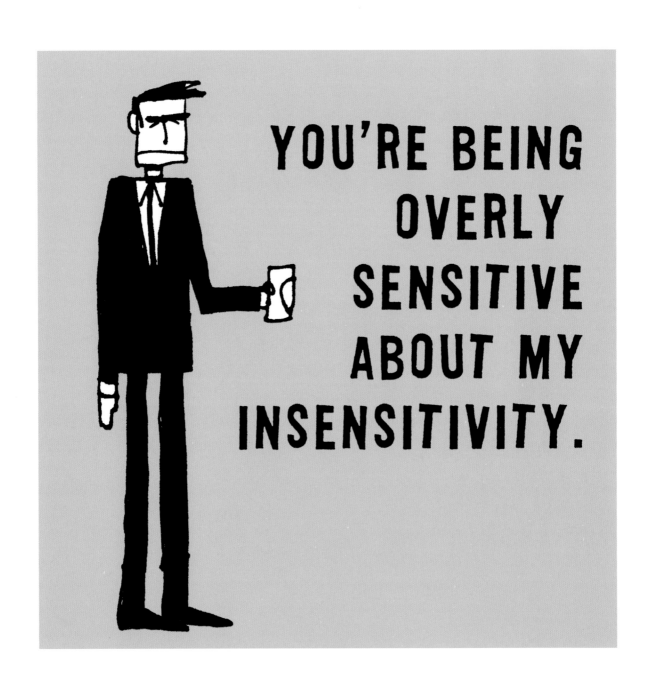

YOU'RE BEING OVERLY SENSITIVE ABOUT MY INSENSITIVITY.

SIMPLY AWESOME.

BEEN THERE.
DRANK THAT.

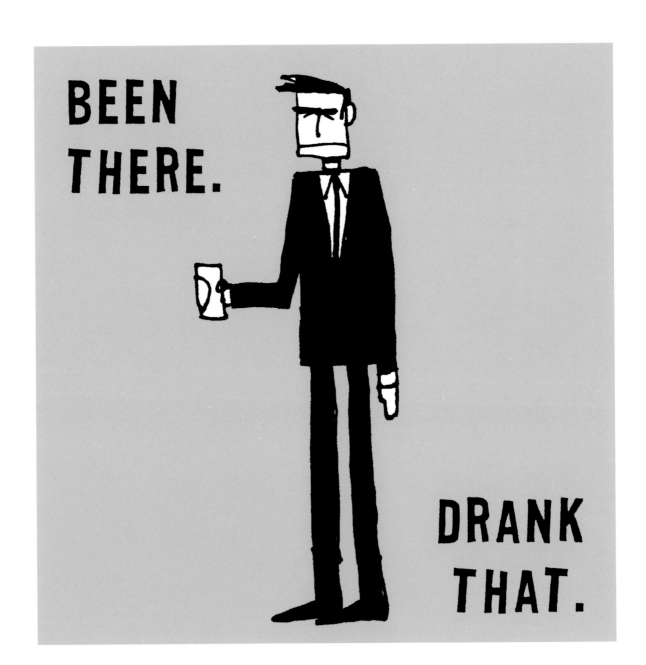

I TEND TO REACT TO MY OWN WEAKNESS WITH STRENGTH.

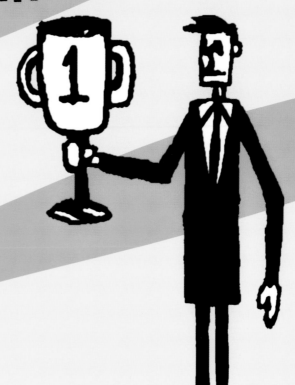

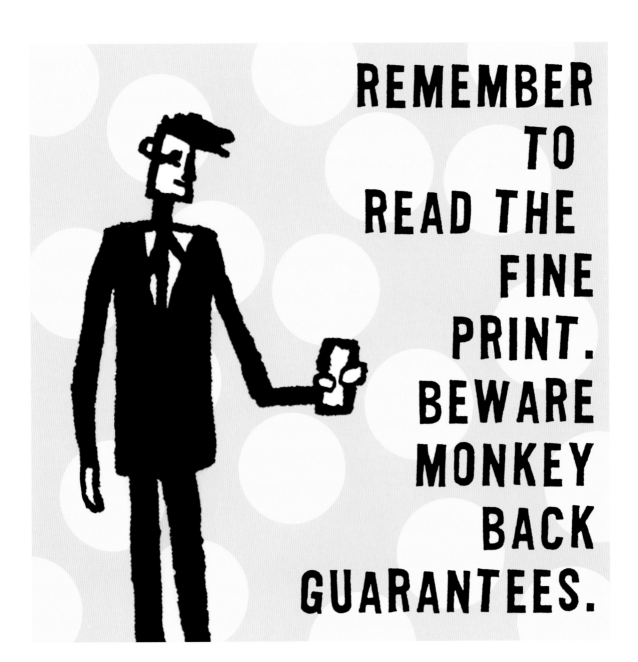

REMEMBER TO READ THE FINE PRINT. BEWARE MONKEY BACK GUARANTEES.

BRING IT.

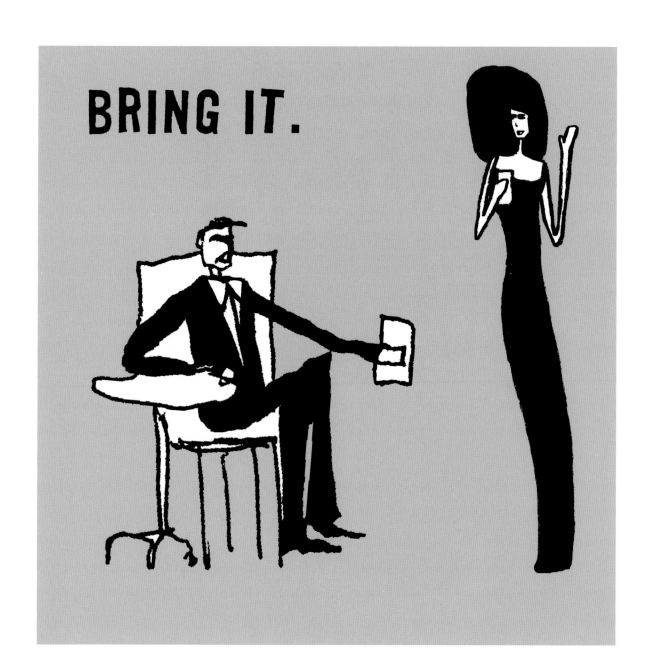

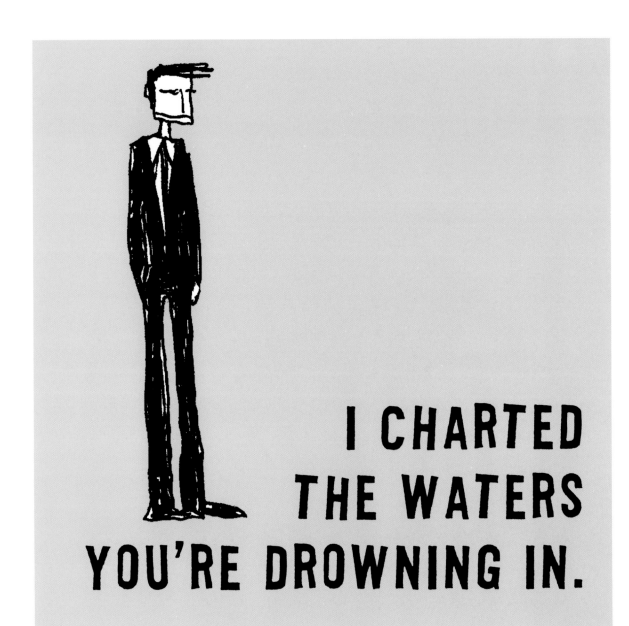

I CHARTED
THE WATERS
YOU'RE DROWNING IN.

WEEKENDS ARE BETTER THAN WEAK BEGINNINGS.

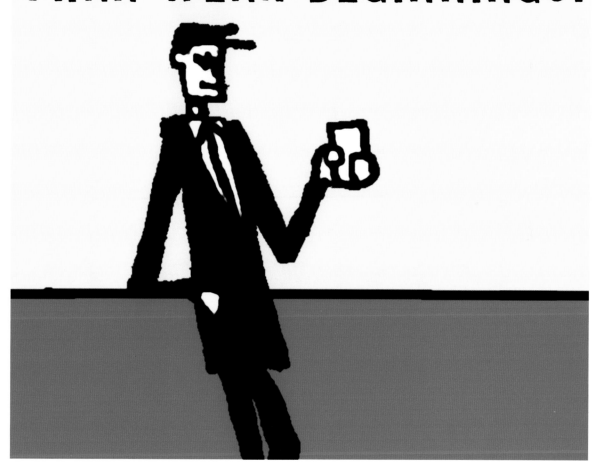

I GOT ANTS IN MY PANTS. I SENSE YOU HAVE CRABS.

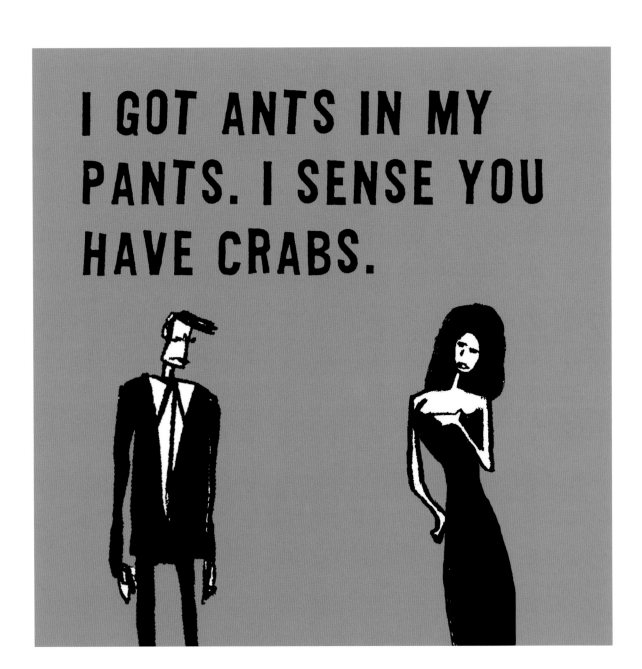

OFFER ME A COSMO, HEAR MY LIVER GIGGLE.

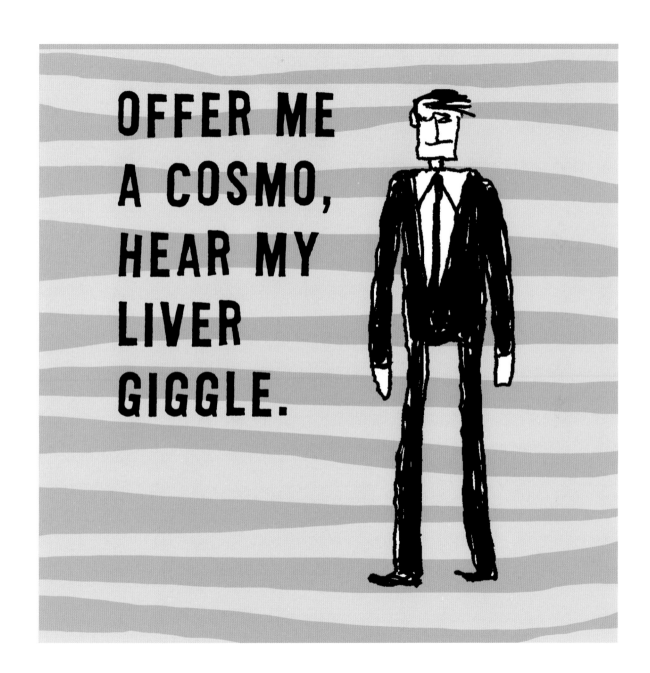

IF YOU WERE ANY DUMBER I'D HAVE TO WATER YOU.

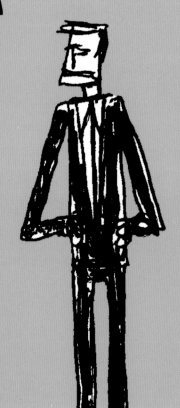

IF YOU
SEE ME
GETTING
SMALLER
THAT
MEANS
YOU'RE
LEAVING.

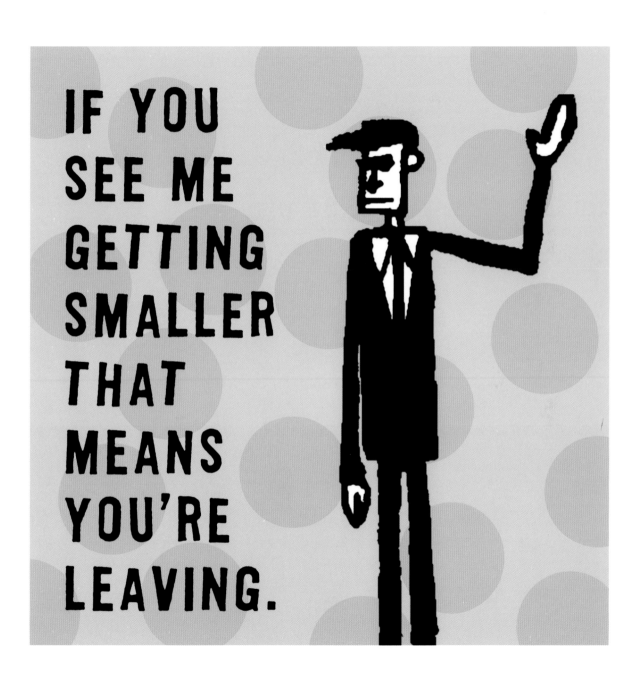

MY EYES WERE BIGGER THAN MY LIVER.

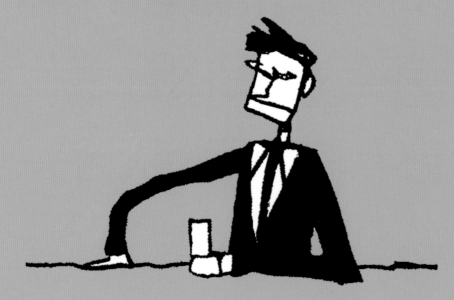

MY DOCTOR ASKED ME IF I WANTED A FLU SHOT. HE WAS HALF RIGHT.

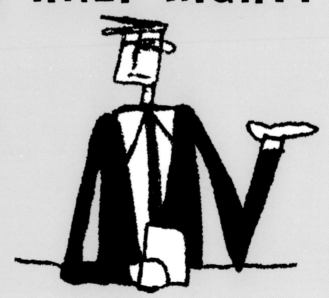

WELL, THIS WASN'T
IN THE GUIDEBOOK.

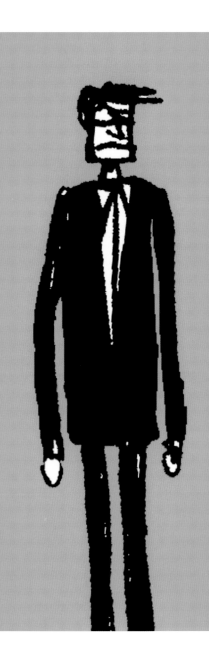

I DON'T NEED A GLASS. IT ALREADY IS IN A GLASS. IT'S CALLED A BOTTLE.

FOUR SCORES
AND
7 SCOTCHES
AGO...

GUILTY
BUT NOT
CHARGED.

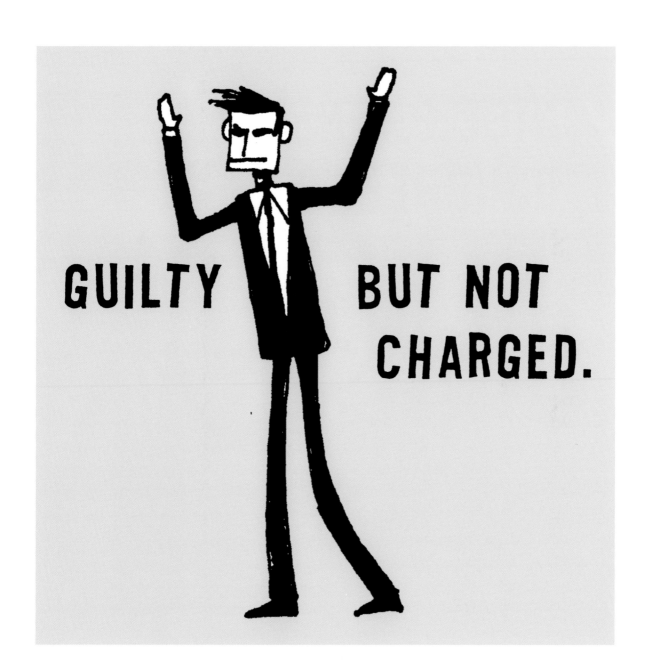

NICE PHONE.
DOUCHEBAG.
1

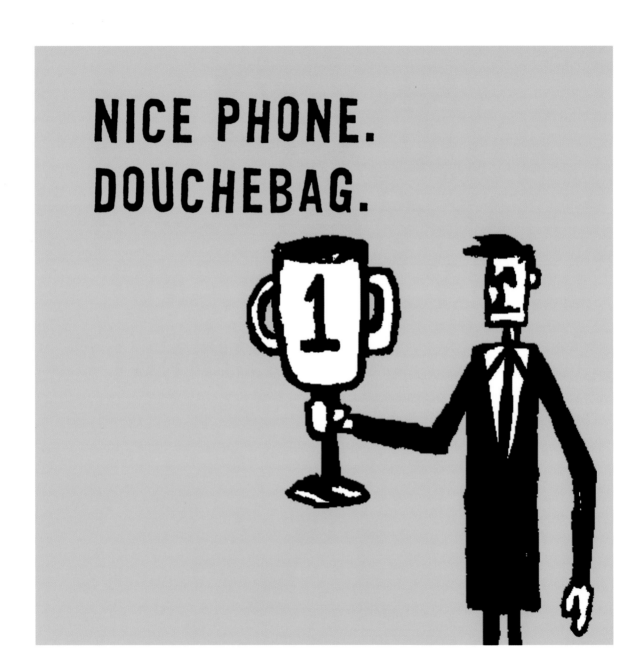

SOBRIETY IS MY HALLOWEEN COSTUME.

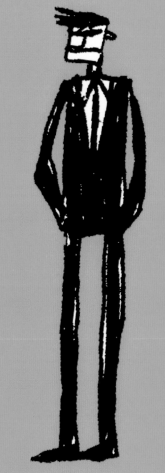

TWITTER.
TEXTING.
POSTING.
IS ANYONE
HERE
ACTUALLY
HERE?

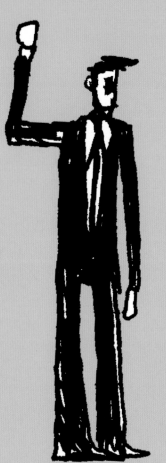

I THOUGHT "WELL-OILED MACHINE" MEANT WE COULD DRINK AT WORK.

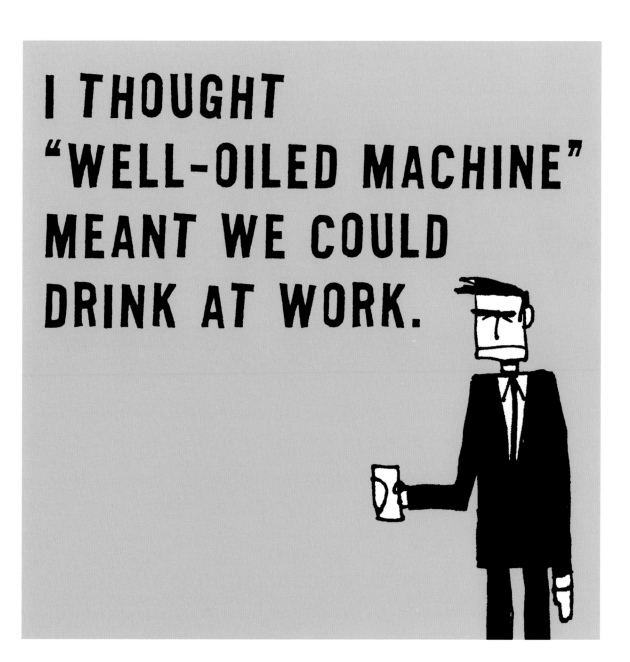

THIS BAR IS MY HOME AWAY FROM MY OTHER BAR.

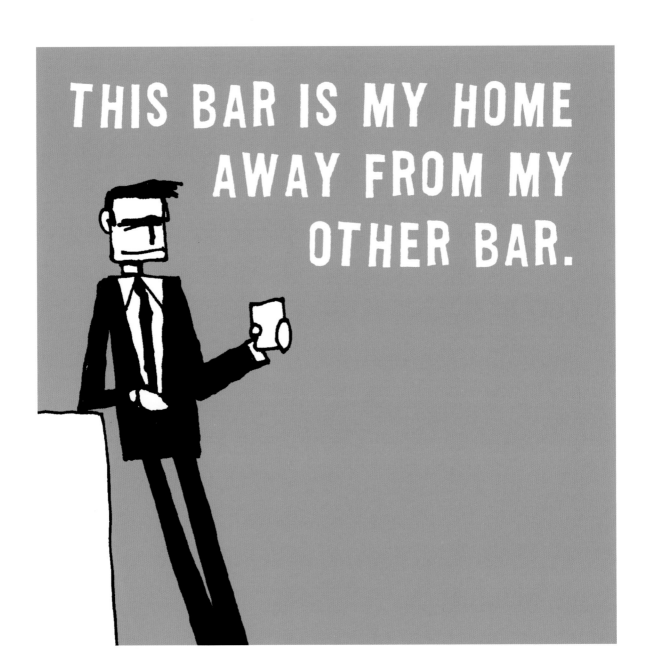

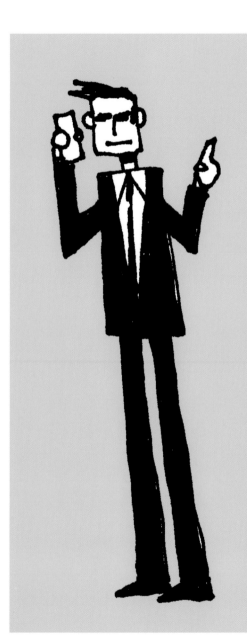

HANG ON, MY DRINK'S CALLING ME.

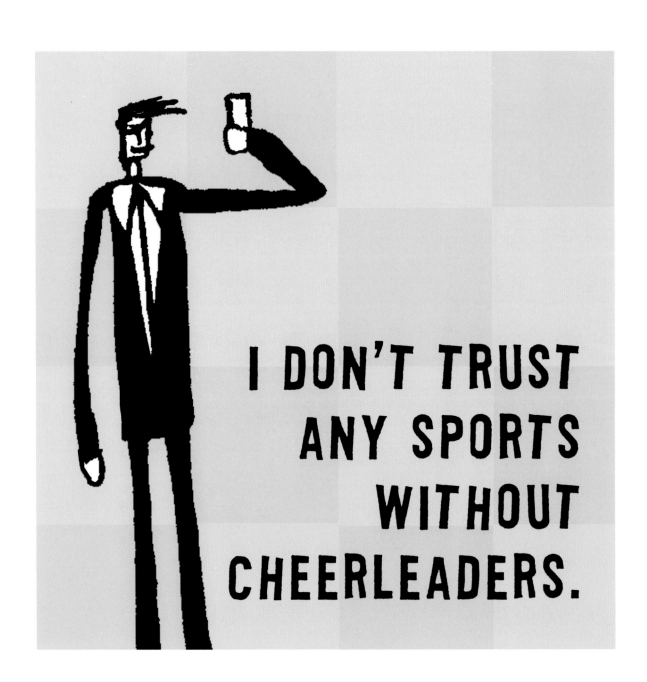

I DON'T TRUST ANY SPORTS WITHOUT CHEERLEADERS.

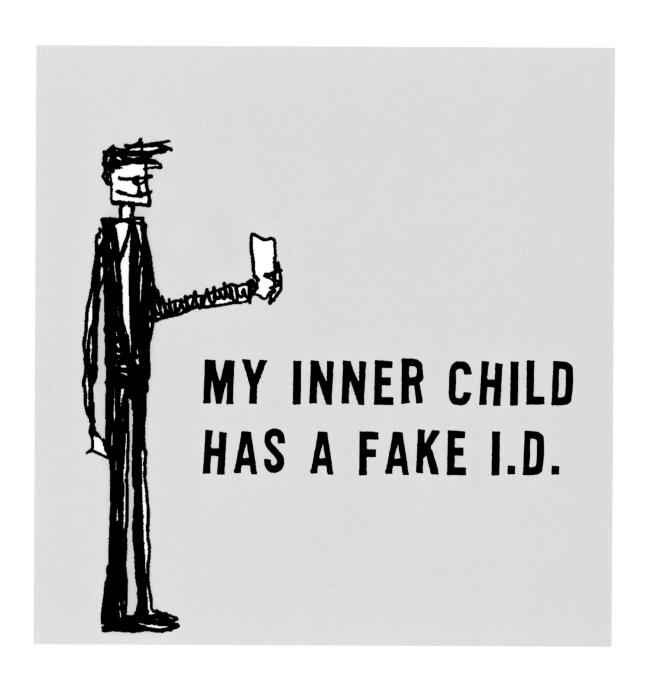

MY INNER CHILD
HAS A FAKE I.D.

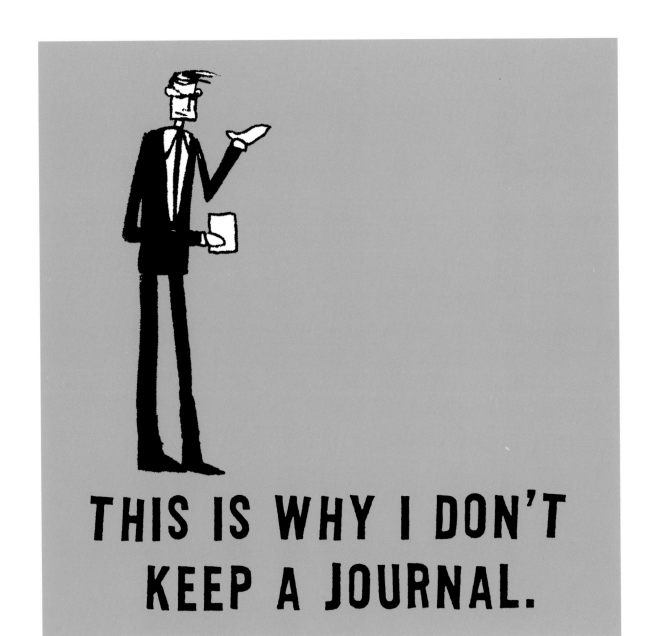

THIS IS WHY I DON'T KEEP A JOURNAL.

I DON'T BELIEVE IN LABELS.
UNLESS THEY'RE FROM PARIS.

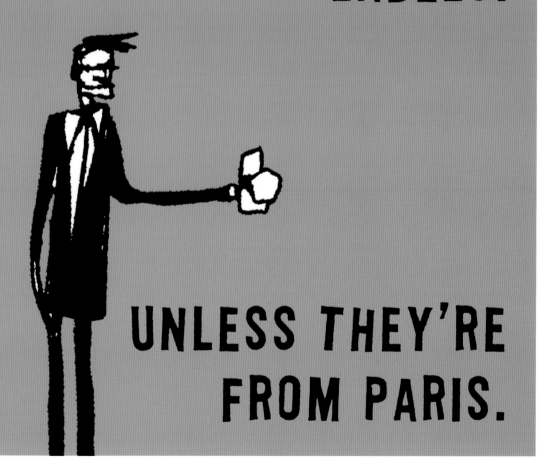

UNTIL IT CAN MAKE
ME A MARGARITA,
NO DOG IS MY
BEST FRIEND.

IF DRINKING KILLS
BRAIN CELLS,
WHY DO I
REMEMBER
MAKING OUT
WITH YOU
LAST NIGHT?

I SHAVED FOR THIS?

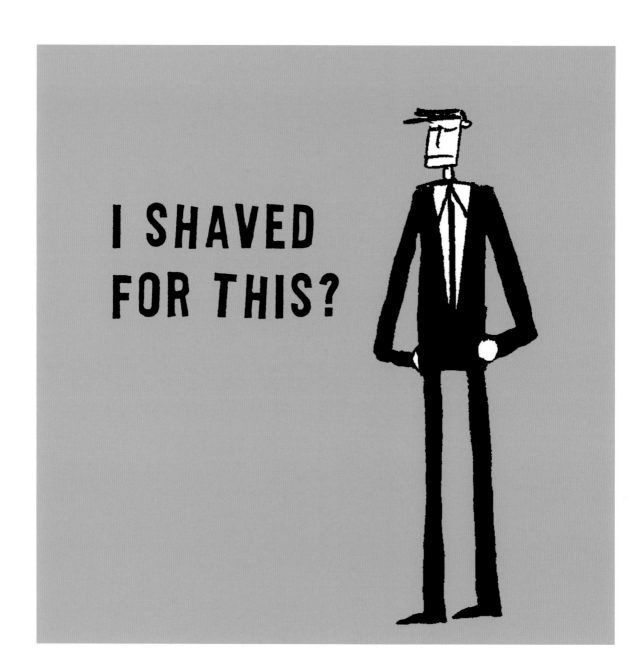

SOME PEOPLE
LIVE IT.
I DRINK IT.

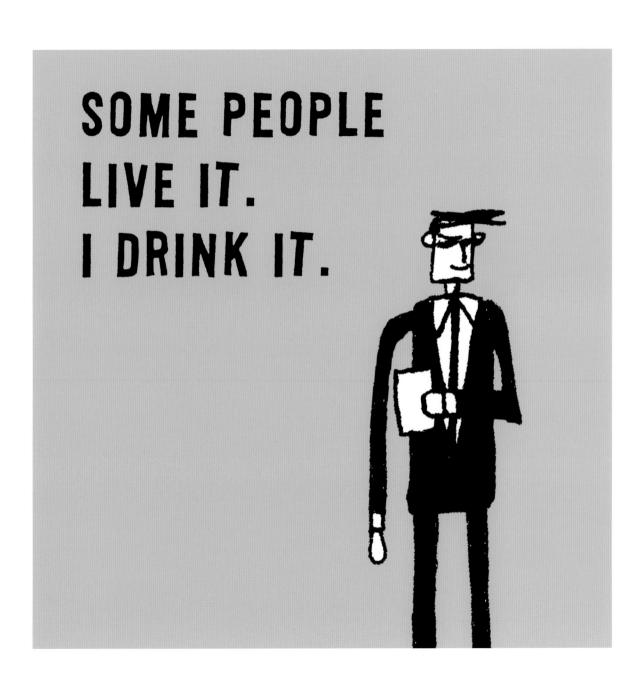

ONE WAY OR
ANOTHER DRINK.

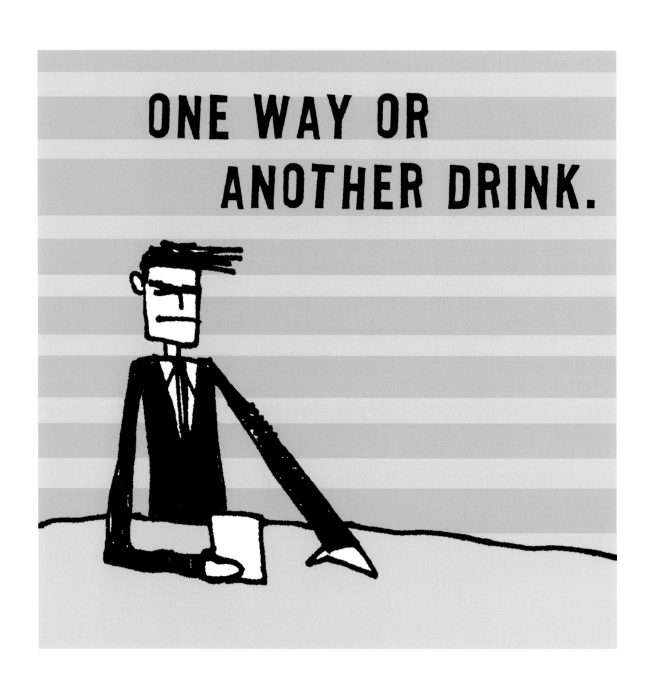

A MONKEY COULD DO MY JOB. HE JUST COULDN'T GET DENTAL INSURANCE.

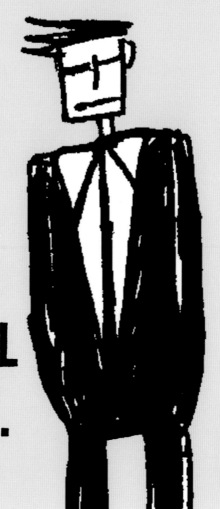

IT'S NOT ME, BABY.
1
IT'S YOU.

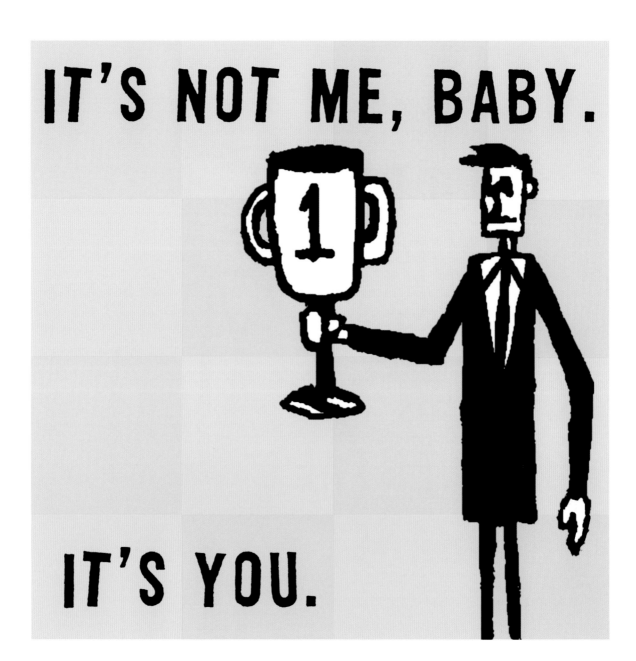

I NAPPED FOR THIS?

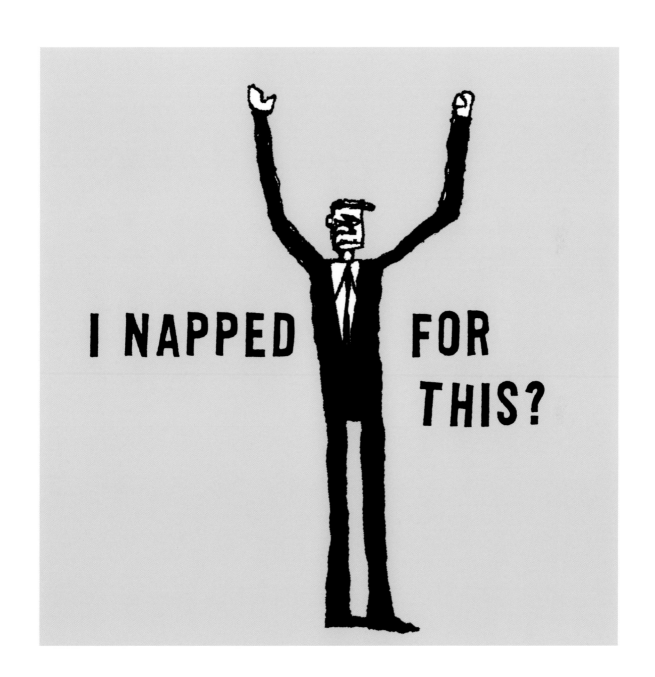

YOU HAD
ME AT
"HAIR OF
THE DOG?"

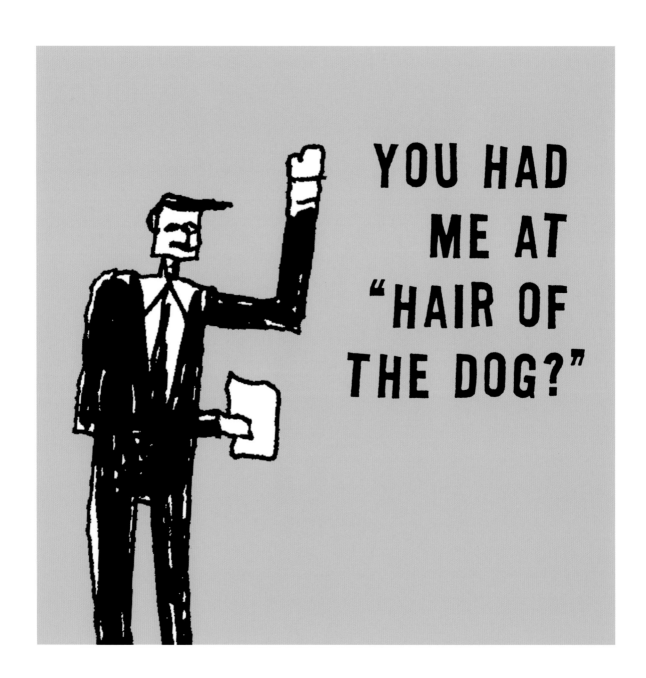

THAT WAS A WASTE OF MY NECK MUSCLES.

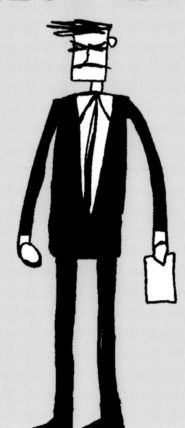

WHAT DO I USUALLY GET HERE?
DRUNK.

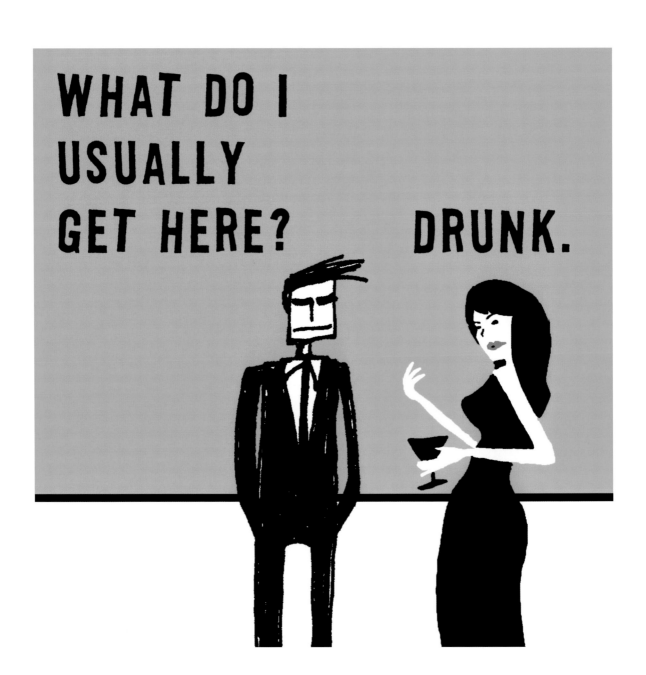

IF YOU DON'T WANT ME TO STARE AT YOUR CHEST, DON'T HOLD YOUR MARTINI NEAR IT.

THERE ARE OTHER FISH OUT THERE. I'M JUST OUT OF HOOKS.

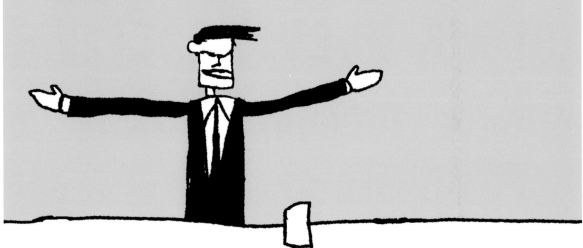

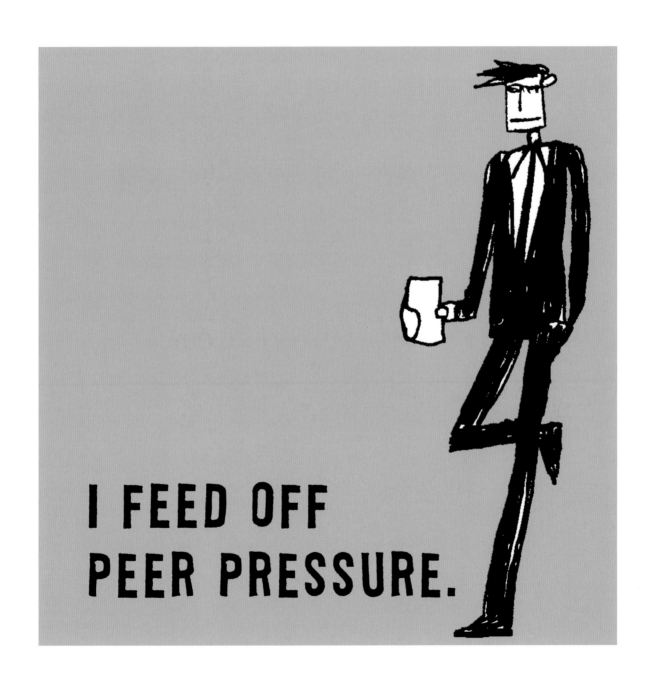

I FEED OFF
PEER PRESSURE.

ARE YOU TWINS
OR AM I
SEEING
DOUBLE?

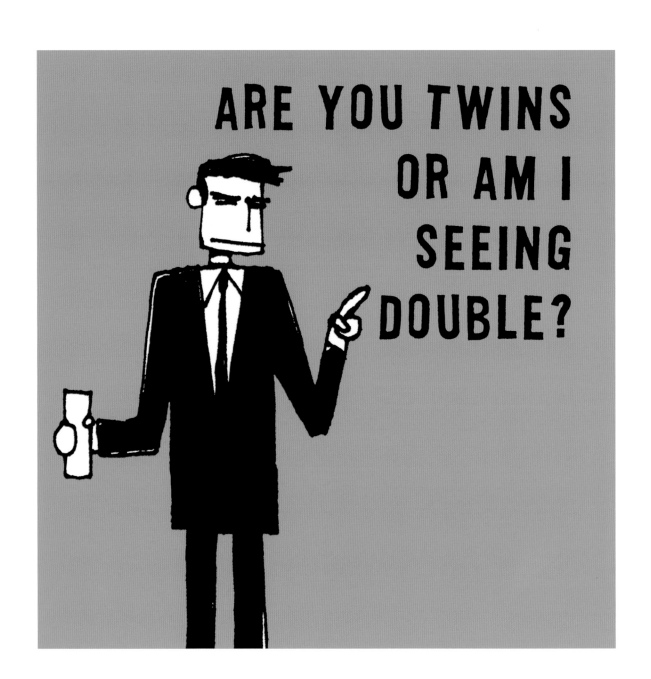

WAS THAT MY OUT LOUD VOICE?

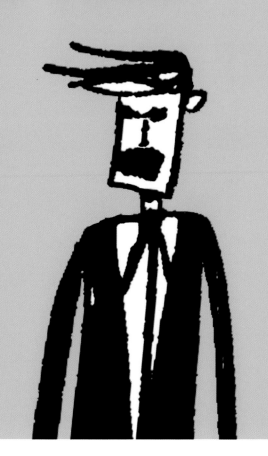

I THINK.
THEREFORE
I DRINK.

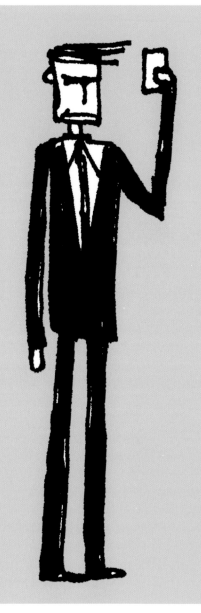

I'M NOT LANDING
PLANES HERE.

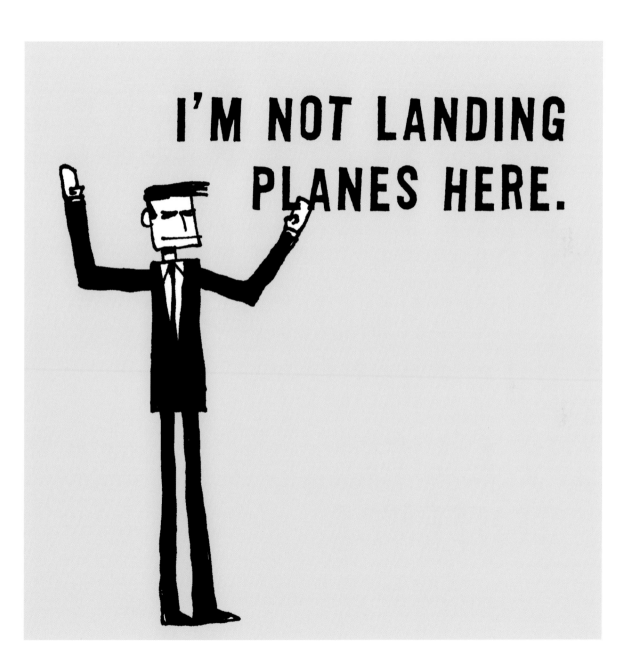

HANGOVERS
CAN FEEL
LIKE
PUNISHMENT.
BUT SOBRIETY
IS A LIFE
SENTENCE.

IT'S NOT RAINING IN HERE. WHY DOES YOUR DRINK HAVE AN UMBRELLA?

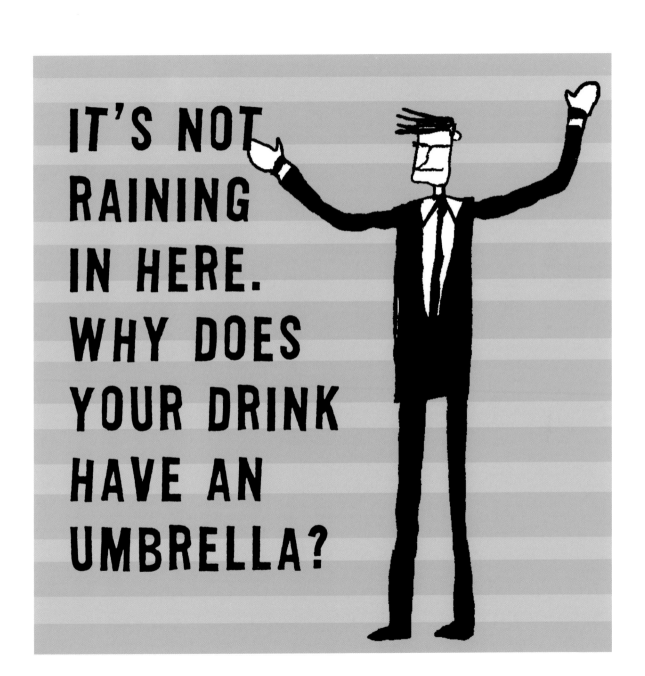

DON'T BUY ROUNDS
FOR
SQUARES.

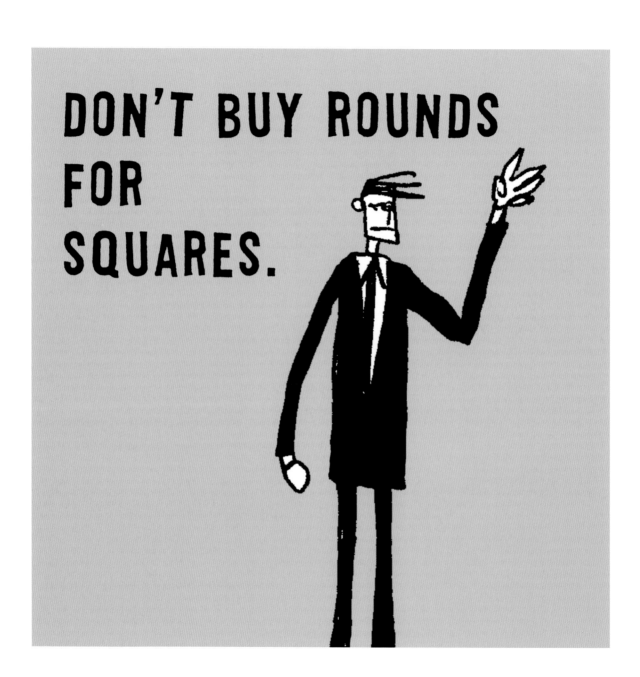

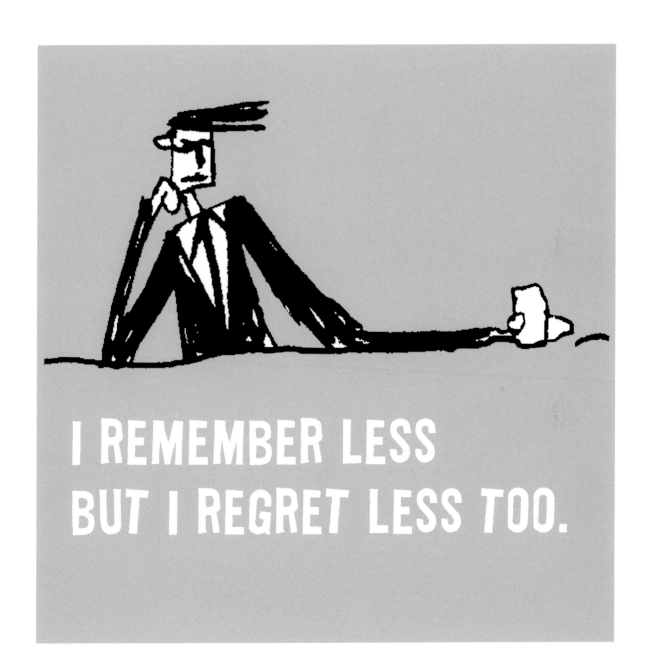

I REMEMBER LESS
BUT I REGRET LESS TOO.

HA-HA FUNNY OR
I NEED TO CALL
MY LAWYER
FUNNY?

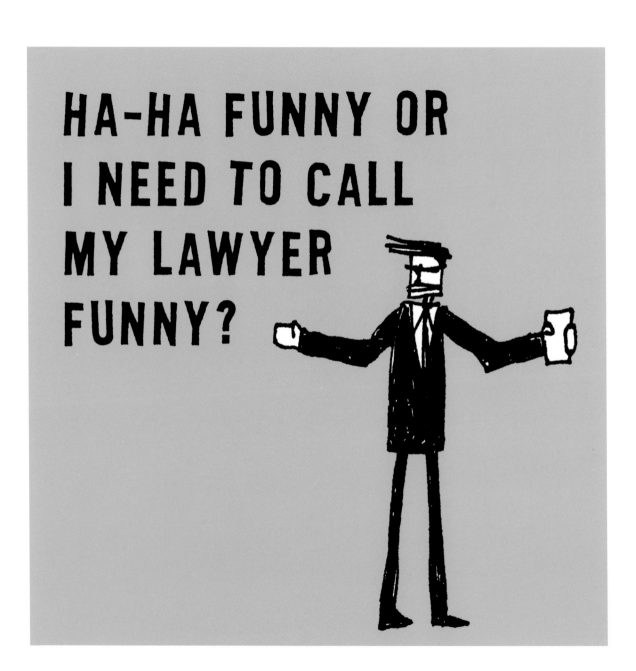

YEAH, I'M THAT GUY,
FROM THAT THING.
DIG IT.

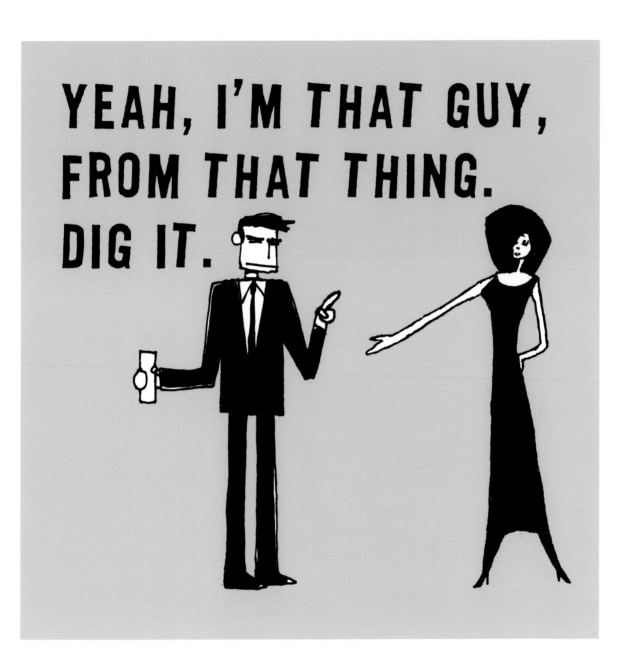

"SHOO."

IT'S LAST CALL.
SOME SETTLING
HAS OCCURRED.

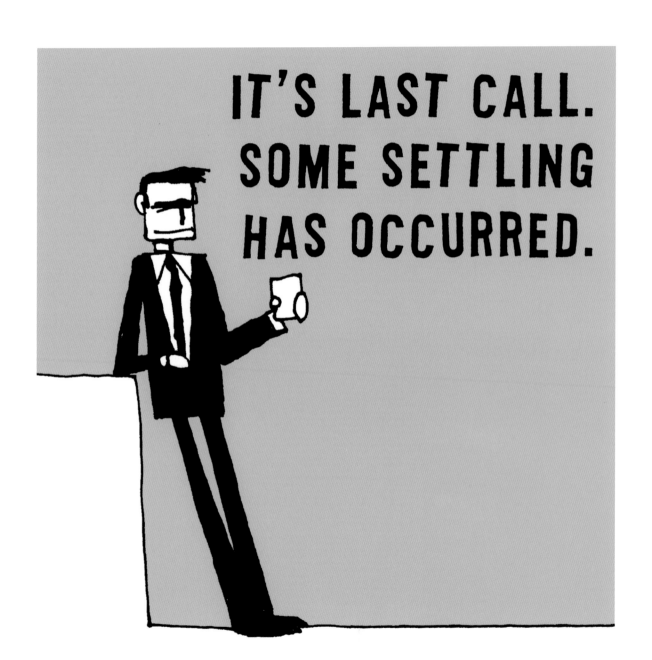

SOME PEOPLE CATCH LIGHTNING IN A BOTTLE.
I DRINK IT.

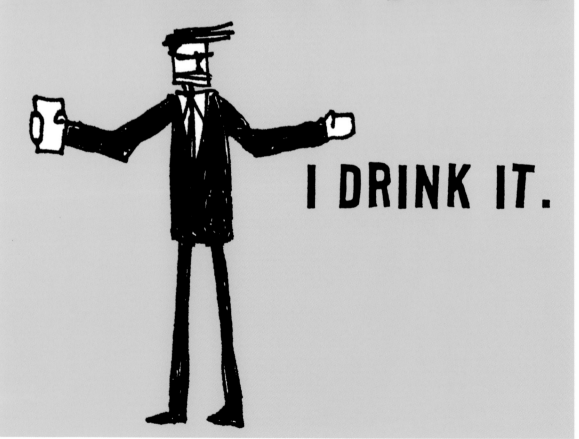

SIT. STAY.
SURE, MY INVISIBLE DOG.

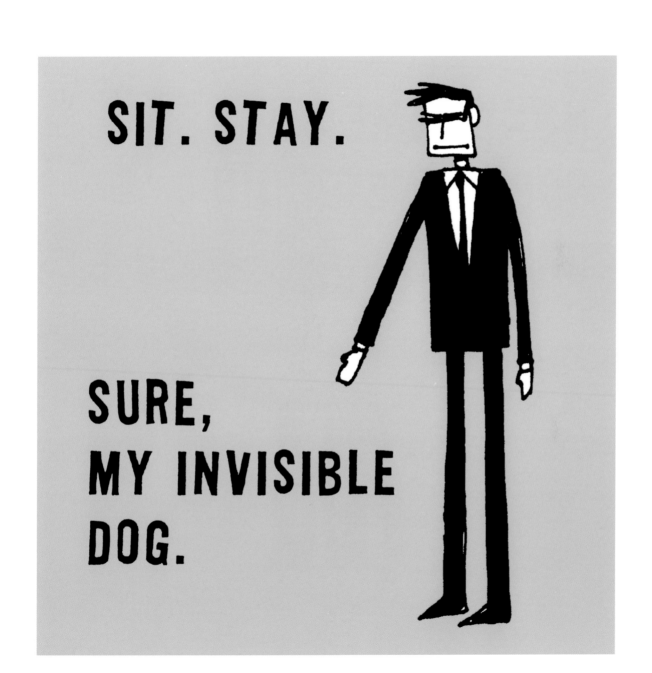

NEXT TIME WE'RE SOBER WE SHOULD DRINK.

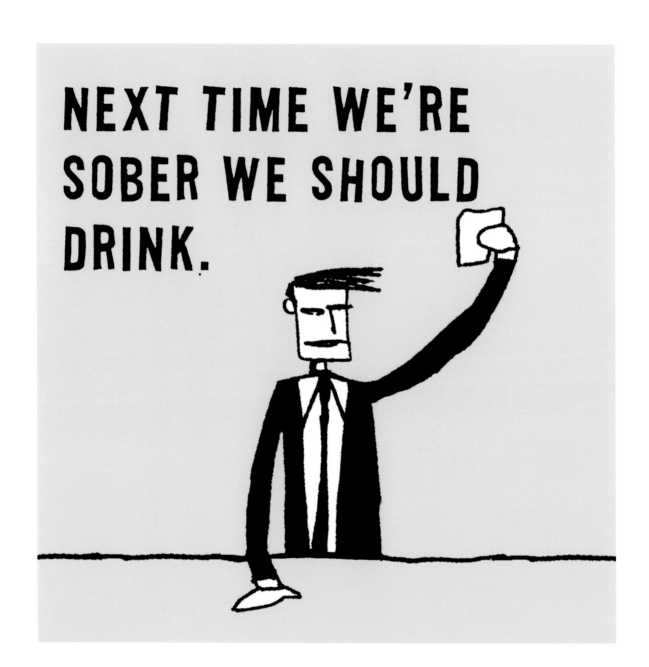

IF MEN ARE FROM MARS AND WOMEN FROM VENUS, THEN EARTH IS SPRING BREAK.

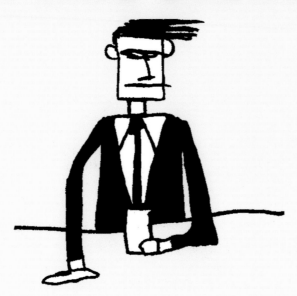

WHEN IT RAINS, POUR.

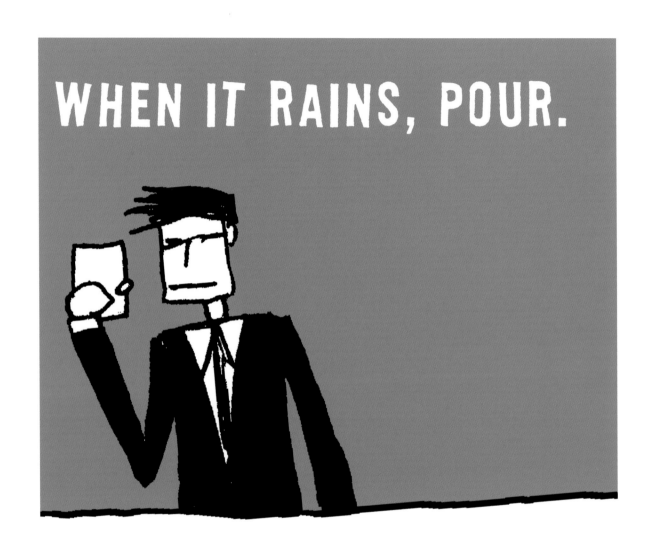

YOU DON'T DRINK TEQUILA.
YOU DO TEQUILA.

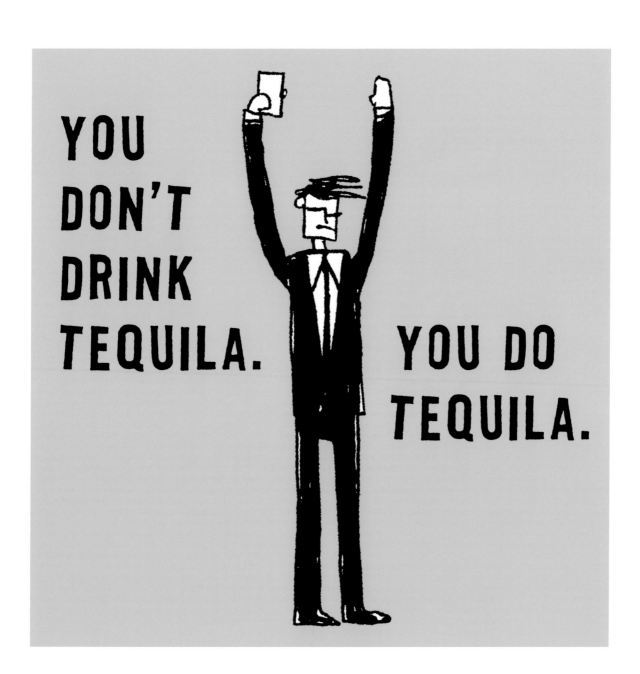

LIVE
FREE
AND
DRINK UP.

THINKING
HARD
WITHOUT
HARDLY
THINKING.

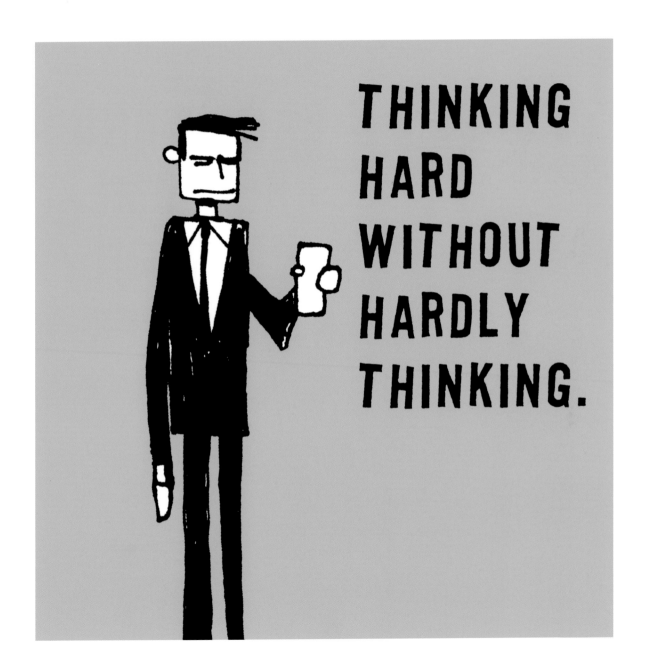

PEACE ON EARTH AND
A THREESOME.
NOT NECESSARILY
IN THAT ORDER.

I LIKE MY SCRAMBLED EGGS SCRAMBLED.

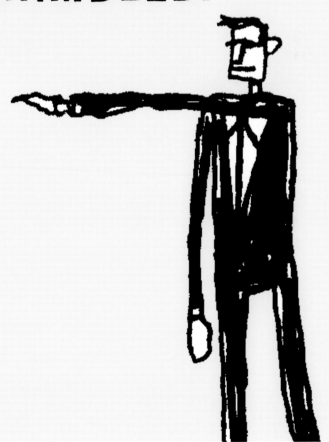

I EAT GUYS LIKE
YOU FOR BREAKFAST.
OR TOAST.

ONE MORE ROUND
AND THEN MY LIVER
ATTACKS
TOKYO.

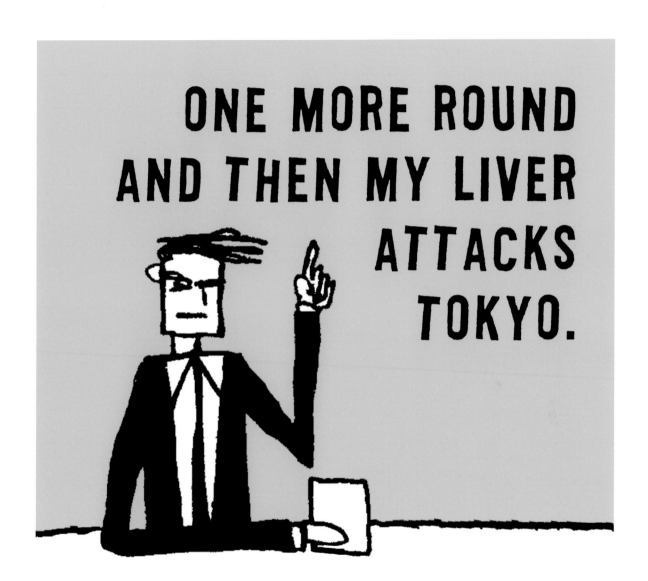

TOP ME
OFF 'TIL I
BOTTOM OUT.

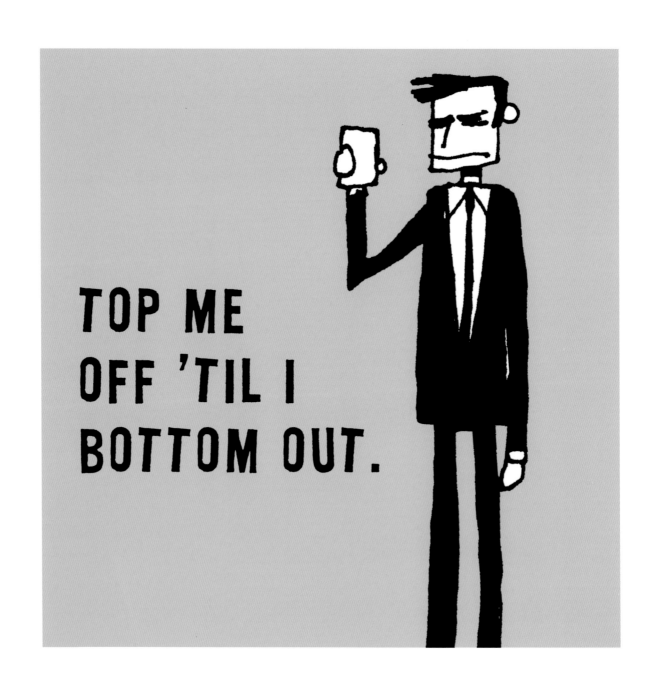

AS SEEN ON TV.

THAT GIRL IS SUPER TIKI.

VAMPIRES DRINK BLOOD.
I JUST DRINK.

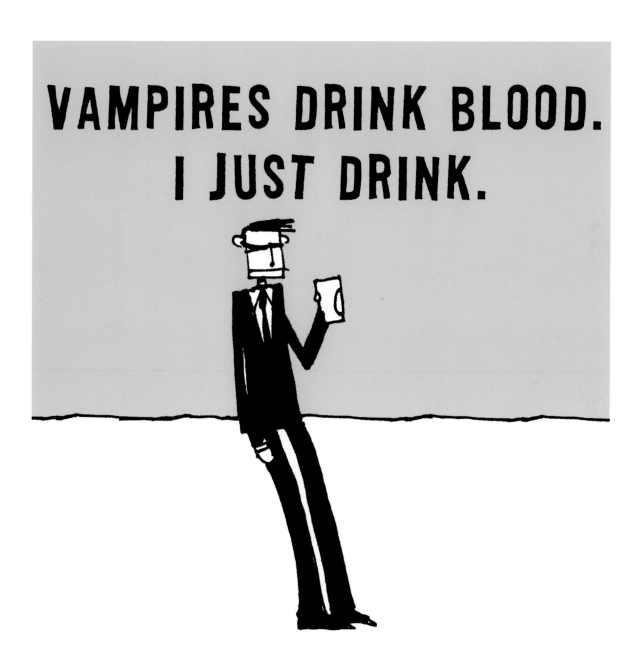

A GOOD TIME FOR
A GOOD TIME.

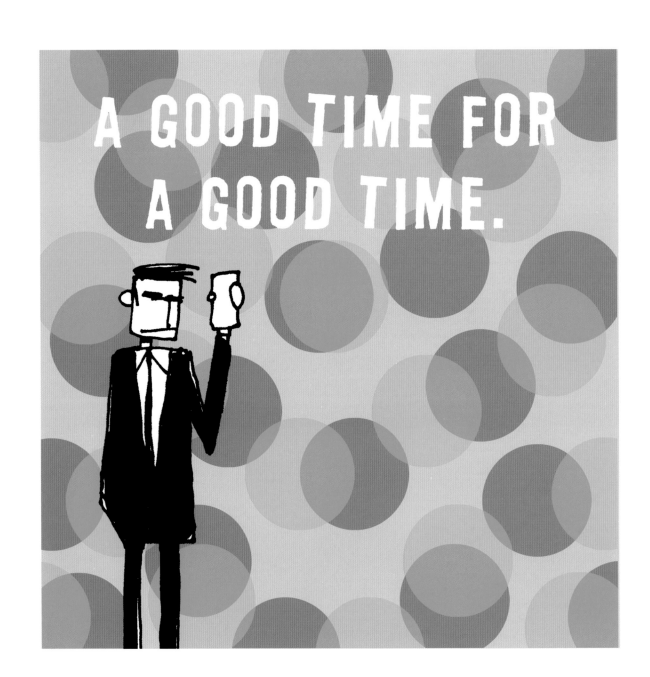

I DON'T KNOW WHY 5 O'CLOCK IS CALLED "QUITTING TIME." THAT'S WHEN I START.

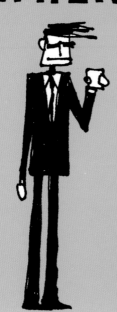

THE ANSWER IS ALWAYS YES.

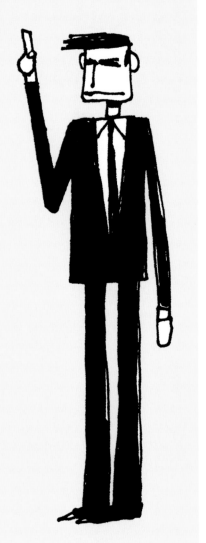